In the Realm of Solace

Bhavana Yoganand

BookLeaf
Publishing

Presentation by *BookLeaf Publishing*

Web: www.bookleafpub.com

E-mail: info@bookleafpub.com

ISBN: 9789357745819

First edition 2023

DEDICATION

I dedicate this book to my loving husband,
adorable children and my whole family.

Abecedarian!

An exciting
 Breaking point,
 Created in havoc,
 Descending reality,
 Episodes unveiling,
 Forging esprit of trust,
 Galloping in the realm of magic,
 Horrors of holy sightings,
 Inciting blissful dreams,
 Journey of anarchy,
 Kindled words,
 Lost in an island,
 Meadows of blunders,
 Nocturnal tinkles,
 Oscillating whispers,
 Preaching winds,
 Quantum of landscape,
 Ravishing with desire,
 Stooping outdoors,
 Treasury of love,
 Upon the lands,
 Vivacious enchantments,
 Waving at me,
 Xylophone melodies,
 Yearnings in
 Zephyr!

Beneath the Shallow Sea!

Let the silent sea swallow,
 Let them sink into the abyss,
 Beneath the waves that churn,
 The complexities of troubled psalm,
 Where creatures swim with grace,
 In the rhythm they find calming salve,
 Let them sink at the ocean's core,
 Beneath the waves, I find the realm,
 Let the ebb flow and hypnotize,
 For there's light in every dark,
 Anchor these sunless musings in the deep,
 Shine beneath from the shallows,
 Where creatures swim in mystic hues,
 For the world above is a rangers nest,
 Let the silent sea swallow,
 The reflections of those struggles,
 And let them drift in waters profound,
 Beneath the waves where stillness reigns!

Dandelion Puffballs!

As I blow the dandelions,
Off goes my anguish along,
The pain of being tied up,
The feeling of distress within,
I let go my anger as I cease them,
A lust for those ruthless desires,
As I blow the dandelions,
I see the tiny hues vanish,
Shades of those envious rupture,
That I built within me,
I see the darkness inside me,
Fading away along with the puffballs,
Bringing in light in my life,
Sailing along with the hope,
Giving raise to the growth in me,
Along with the courage from within
To heal and evolve with perseverance,
To evoke with love and endurance,
As I gain the Sun's power and preserve,
As I blow the dandelions,
I rejoice cherishing my preadolescence!

A Perfect Mug of Chai!

A Chai mug filled with essence,
Pastels, rosy and matcha flavored,
They're soaked in vanilla spice,
And crystals of lemongrass oil,
I was psyched by the rosemary tinge,
My thoughts woke me up last night,
Poems that I could fill my notes,
Words popped up and I started scribing,
My cup of magic I made, helped me,
My mind just sparked upon some lines,
I penned about angels in the spectre,
I wrote about the windy vulnerabilities,
I thought about you when I was awake,
Wide open eyes of mine hints for a prattle,
About the pitch dark sky, with rainy clouds,
I was waiting for the midnight raindrops,
And the stars in your eyes, that glow,
On your face to see a faint smile,
Let's share a cup of chai,
You see it's my magic potion,
They're filled with esthetic essence,
Perfect for just you and me!

Mirror Mirror on the wall!

A child within me,
 Always wanting to see,
 Happy face with big smile,
 Oh! Mirror Mirror on the wall,
 Who do you think is cutest of all?
 Would it be me, coz I have it all?
 Nature's spice, angel's voice,
 Sweet as a sugar, with a choice,
 You already know, my name is Joyce,
 The one who is sharp and witty,
 The one who is strong and pretty,
 And belongs to the old town city,
 It's dark here, but I can see,
 I can see droplets of glee,
 Filled with emotions at spree,
 I see your paws, they're filed,
 To hunt me down you're obliged,
 I know that you're really psyched,
 With a look that is truly fake,
 And with a eyes that is Blake,
 It's tough to give you a break,
 I can sense I'm in a peril,
 Alas! I feel at a safe level,
 Coz you no longer seem a devil,
 My sad faces have gone,

I know I will soon abscond,
And you will be easily conned!

A Pacifist!

She is a portrait of pain,
 Modeling her moods to his moods,
 Acrimonious, yet a pacifist,
 Swinging hopes with withered eyes,
 Her amethyst sigh spoke phrases,
 The essence of midnight tremors,
 Sultry sighs and lurking pain,
 Swinging hopes of forlorn dreams,
 She is a portrait of pain,
 In echoes of tranquility he lived,
 Her lucent eyes igniting frozen heart,
 Her twilight memories find me,
 Despite the viles of transparency,
 Gracing the first sight of calmness,
 When she said with a graceful node,
 Embracing herself to wither from within,
 I am so lost in you... with her faint voice,
 He was psyched from her fervor cues,
 She is a portrait of pain,
 Acrimonious, yet a pacifist!!

You will always be remembered!

May be you're in a better place than here,
May be this was the way you had to go,
But still, my heart feels heavy and filled,
With a burst of emotions and tears,
Those tears which is hidden deep inside,
That is looking for a way to pour out,
The exact same day I last spoke to you,
6 years apart, but still so fresh it stays,
You're the soul that took a special place,
In my heart, you will always be,
I know I made a lot of mistakes,
When you were here I never realized them,
But will you ever be able to forgive me?
My dear Grandma, you are the best,
I got so much that I can still learn from you,
Will you still teach me the thing I need?
I love you and I will always love you,
You will always be a special person to me,
A soul who was always so selfless and sweet,
I love you and I will always love you!

She's a Mother!

She who's an angel on Earth,
She who wears invisible wings,
She who brings a soul to life,
She who teaches a soul to live,
She's the first teacher,
One who teaches her child to smile,
One who teaches that crying isn't bad,
The one who witnesses joy,
In every little steep her baby takes,
A 'Mother' she is given a name,
A soul who replicates selflessness,
The one who never gets tired,
Of the tantrums thrown by her child,
A gentle touch of hers is a blessing,
A few minutes of nap on her lap,
Feels like a long hour of sleep,
In her arms is where there's the world,
A place where her child feels safe
She's a Mother who's an angel,
She's a Mother who's a blessing!!

A Born Cancerian!

A fiery Cancerian,
Born with the traits to surrender,
To relinquish the joy of being a warrior,
And to stay strong during hurdles,
To stay grounded during success,
And, to be passionate about triumphs,
Learning to conquer my weakness,
And to counter those strengths,
My attributes are those,
That fit the best with fire,
I'm the one who survives,
As strong as the puff of breeze,
As sharp as the first morning rays,
An element of Mother Earth who's fierce,
And the aspects that match with nature,
My failures don't frighten me,
They help me mold and reshape my life,
Binding me within the roots of emotions,
She! who is a dominant soul,
She! who knows to rule, and she,
Who knows her bounds in the cosmos!

He Waits!

The dawn of the day,
Quite seemed like a treasure,
With orangish-yellow rays,
As the sky was fully lit,
To spread light through its pace,
Mr.Sun who was waiting for us,
To start our day afresh,
With bright blooms and glooms,
As we get busy throughout the day,
He is still there, still shining alone,
Not tired at all waits up there,
Be it at the first-morning meal,
Or at the meridian supper,
He now is a tad bit tired,
When it's almost time for some coffee,
He soon is seen to move his pace,
Almost about to bid a goodbye,
His day is about to end,
At so is ours- like he always reminds us,
When it's almost time for chow,
He's gone to sleep and end his day,
When the dusk is fallen,
And it now looks so dark around,
With only one shiny satellite,
Who never fails to orbit the planet,

He who doesn't lose his glow,
Mostly seen with some sparkling stars,
And there is a wait for dusk again!

Moonless Nights!

There's no clear sky,
Nor is there veils of brightness,
All I can sense is a silent roar,
Stronger than that of a cougar,
Everywhere is covered with russet hue,
Ariel view with sonic crystal clear dew,
Fading stars and moonless nights,
Filled with snow cold winter sight,
A deadly dusk with vampire screams,
A howl that couldn't be heard too far,
Alas! It felt as if it was a wounding scar,
That was left behind by the prey of silence,
Fading stars and moonless nights,
Ahead of the timeless lesion,
I fear the end of refulgence,
Envisioning the aura of a presense,
That which is the future,
That which is bound further,
Scare that spread across the miles,
Belief that it will just be the lies,
Diamond dusts all around me,
With a mere creation of bounty,
Hunting down with frequent melody,
It was silent night under the sky,
With a hope that there was an alibi,
Breezy clime by the end of friday!

Lighthouse shows directions!

In the fields where grasses were green,
Somewhere in the mere location of meadows,
Cows grazing at the endless pastures,
I stood there admiring their flair,
As I began walking, marching ahead of me,
I looked at the azure sky, much farther away,
The passing clouds that had weird shapes,
I started imagining them to take forms,
Some like that of the cotton candy,
Some like that of the waving flag,
Some like that of a mountain peak,
And some like that of an ocean's wave,
I walked further and further,
That's when I got tired and sat down,
I was surprised to see the color changing,
From Green to red, red to yellow,
From yellow to amber and from amber to green,
I was wondering what could it be,
That could change it's color aquiring nature,
A chameleon that passed from one place to another,
So creepy yet so beautifully created,
I was thirsty and now I wanted to quench,
A pond with crystal clear water, so fresh,
I walked and walked again until it was dark,

There stood the lighthouse, so tall a structure,
That is believed to show directions to a
wanderer!

We all prosper!

With rugged scraps life battles,
A bare brokenness of rags,
Tattered cloth with untold sagas,
Unkept and worn from many drags,
A sight that leaves us in agas,

Once a garment of great worth,
Now reduced to mere shreds on earth,
Its fabric tells us of the by gone days,
Of struggles fought, and tears we cried.
Of what we lost and what we didn't find,

Yet, in its frayed and in oddment state,
A beauty hides that's hard to rate,
For in its very brokenness,
Lies a story of great fondness,
Without any need of wickedness,

A tale of love that never fades,
Of memories that time cascades,
A bond that stands the test of age,
And a spirit that never fades,
Beyond the life with many crusades,

Even when there's so much to resist,

Let us just not dismiss the rags,
That lie before our very eyes,
For in its bare brokenness,
A beauty hides that which never dies!

From the shallows to the shadows,
Let us rate those mighty tales,
With no hesitation we make riches,
With perspire we make progress,
Rags to riches, we all prosper!

A Moonchild!

I am a moonchild,
 Defined by my anomalies,
 In the serendipity that I live in,
 I cherish the most diverse judgments,
 Always the one believing in,
 And living in reality checks,
 For if dreams die,
 The fire of life dies along,
 I always believed that,
 Love is a smoke made with,
 The fumes of sighs,
 We pretend to smile at every turmoil,
 And shy away at every stranger faced,
 A resolute of decisions we make,
 Singularity in our diverse mind,
 Putting together to be one of a kind,
 Euphoria in my soul,
 When I feel connected to,
 The treasures of this world,
 Without being held back from within,
 To sail, to shine, and to share!

At the touch of Love!

A story I didnt want to title, oddly in the artistic life,
 As I fuel my devotion, like a master pionist playing,
 I am healing everyday, from the dust I emerge,
 The memories that never mend in the burnt orange skies,
 Our dreams get smaller, but our hopes never cease,
 The cosmos of burning emblishments exist precisely,
 Poems from the typewriter are the last letter,
 From your lover- because you are my better half now,
 Poetry according to poets; are in line between sanity and madness,
 While my ode to you, maybe in next life,
 Will look like an empty notebook with invisible messages,
 For they say, at the touch of love, everyone becomes a poet!

An Acrostic on TREASURE!

Tiny monents that add
Remarkably
Enchanting values,
Achievably the best and
Sweet memories that
Unanimously incite
Refreshing cocktails of
Ecstasy in ardor!

I am a Fortune cookie

I unfold many beliefs,
 Wisdom about the future,
I tell predictions,
Talk about your fate,
The mysteries of unknown,
I ramble thoughts within,
For the fortune,
I need to sell,
You wouldn't believe all in me,
But, I must tell,
Tales about you, for sure,
Found in Chinese restaurants,
From kids to adults,
All love me, xoxo,
May be because its fun,
To pull a strip out of me,
With scribbled messages,
Which you feel may not be true,
Or may be you can make it real,
I am a fortune cookie,
Baked in a unique shape,
I talk about your future,
As if I know you very well,
I am a fortune cookie,
With an intriguing mystery!

O, Bunnies of Easter!

O, Bunnies of Easter,
 Laying eggs of Color,
 Spreading love and cheer!

O, the children, amid Easter,
 Carrying little baskets,
 Putting their cute smiles,
 Off to hunt those eggs,

O, the people, when Easter,
 Dressing up all way,
 Munching on savory,
 Gather with family.

O Bunnies of Easter,
 Laying eggs of color,
 O, the children, amid Easter,
 Are off to hunt those eggs!

Dear Poet!

I write the words of wisdom,
 Deep thoughts evoke meaning;
 My quest for illusions grow,
 My frame of mind invoked;
 Enlightening sketches and actions;
 The ink etches my soul,
 Writing my selfless tales;
 Commotion in my senses;
 I write words of magic,
 To create a leap of luck!
 I am a poetess of my spirit,
 Casting the spell of love!
 Dear poet, I wrote this poem for you,
 With my heart, soul and mind!
 You're the kind I always aspire to be!
 I am a poetess of my spirit!
 Says my soul to you,
 For you and me are unified,
 Unified with the same notions,
 Dear poet, I wrote this poem for you,
 In this glorious magical world!!

Kindness in words!

A melody that lingers like a soothing balm,
Your overflowing kindness is like a psalm,
Your presence is like a breath of fresh air,
Your care and love are beyond compare,
A singing beacon who is a guiding star,
Thank you for being who you truly are,
Kindness brimming from your soul,
Everflowing kindness, your treasure trove,
In a world where kindness is rare,
Your hues of love and warmth is flair,
I see the beauty enticing in your eyes,
Soothing presence of happiness in disguise,
In a spring's garden you're blooming flower,
In a mellowed harmony, you're an embower,
A moment of sight of your beauty enticing,
A rare composition of your heart thriving,
You're bold and beautiful, a true friend,
In a nature's palace you're a mere blend!

Lies tangle, Truth frees!

Deceived with fame game played,
Daggered with a double edged sword,
A soul caught in the trap of design,
Falsehood that's vowen with thread,
Estranged with false promises,
Lies that are tangled with emotions,
Where truth is not valued with time,
Beware of the tangled web of lies,
Deception spins it's intricate web,
And soon they become ensnared,
In a world that can be ruthless,
Tangled in the cobweb of lies,
Leaving behind the labyrinths,
Being not able to get rid of it,
Finding a way out would vanquish,
But there will be a day to come,
Where truth will break free,
There will be a sudden upheaval,
Where in the world that's ruthless,
A disguise that always attracts,
Falsehood that woves a thread,
A connection that always hinders,
Honesty would take over falsity,
The world would be a better place,
To live, love and rejoice with peace,

Where connections can be believed,
And there's no more cobweb of lies,
To value the authenticity of emotions!